A DISSERTA ON SLAVER WITH A PROPOSAL FOR THE GRADUAL ABOLITION OF IT, IN THE STATE OF VIRGINIA

BY ST. GEORGE TUCKER

AUTHOR WAS PROFESSOR OF LAW IN THE UNIVERSITY OF WILLIAM AND MARY, AND ONE OF THE JUDGES OF THE GENERAL COURT, IN VIRGINIA.

Slavery not only violates the Laws of Nature, and of civil Society, it also wounds the best Forms of Government: in a Democracy, where all Men are equal, Slavery is contrary to the Spirit of the Constitution.

MONTESQUIEU.

PHILADELPHIA:

PRINTED FOR MATHEW CAREY,

No. 118, Market-Street.

1796.

TO THE

General Assembly of Virginia,

To whom it belongs to decide upon the expediency and practicability of a plan for the *gradual abolition* of *Slavery* in this commonwealth,

The following pages are most respectfully submitted and inscribed,

BY THE AUTHOR.

Williamsburg, in Virginia,

May 20, 1796.

TO THE READER.

The following pages form a part of a course of Lectures on Law and Police, delivered in the University of William and Mary, in this commonwealth. The Author considering the Abolition of Slavery in this State, as an object of the first importance, not only to our moral character and domestic peace, but even to our political salvation; and being persuaded that the accomplishment of so momentous and desirable an undertaking will in great measure depend upon the early adoption of some plan for that purpose, with diffidence submits to the consideration of his countrymen his ideas on a subject of such consequence. He flatters himself that the plan he ventures to suggest, is liable to fewer objections than most others that have been submitted to the consideration of the public, as it will be attended with a gradual change of condition in the blacks, and cannot possibly affect the interest either of creditors, *or any other description of persons of the* present generation: *and posterity he makes no doubt will feel themselves relieved from a perilous and grievous burden by the timely adoption of a plan, whose operation may be felt by them, before they are borne down by a weight which threatens destruction to our happiness both public and private.*

☞ The following ADDITIONAL NOTES have been received from the Author since the body of this work was printed off.

In page 20, after the word arms, *in line 5, read this note:*

This was the case under the laws of the state; but the Act of 2. Cong. c. 33. for establishing an uniform militia throughout the United States, seems to have excluded all but free white men from bearing arms in the militia.

To the word slave, *page 47, line 14, add the following note:*

It may not be improper here to note, that the first congress of the United States, at their third session, Dec. 1793, passed an act to prohibit the carrying on the slave trade from the United States to any foreign place or country; the provisions of which seem well calculated to restrain the citizens of united America from embarking in so infamous a traffick.

ON THE
STATE OF SLAVERY IN VIRGINIA.

In the preceding Enquiry[1] into the absolute rights of the citizens of united America, we must not be understood as if those rights were equally and universally the privilege of all the inhabitants of the United States, or even of all those, who may challenge this land of freedom as their native country. Among the blessings which the Almighty hath showered down on these states, there is a large portion of the bitterest draught that ever flowed from the cup of affliction. Whilst America hath been the land of promise to Europeans, and their descendants, it hath been the vale of death to millions of the wretched sons of Africa. The genial light of liberty, which hath here shone with unrivalled lustre on the former, hath yielded no comfort to the latter, but to them hath proved a pillar of darkness, whilst it hath conducted the former to the most enviable state of human existence. Whilst we were offering up vows at the shrine of Liberty, and sacrificing hecatombs upon her altars; whilst we swore irreconcilable hostility to her enemies, and hurled defiance in their faces; whilst we adjured the God of Hosts to witness our resolution to live free, or die, and imprecated curses on their heads who refused to unite with us in establishing the empire of freedom; we were imposing upon our fellow men, who differ in complexion from us, a *slavery*, ten thousand times more cruel than the utmost extremity of those grievances and oppressions, of which we complained. Such are the inconsistencies of human nature; such the blindness of those who pluck not the beam out of their own eyes, whilst they can espy a moat, in the eyes of their brother; such that partial system of morality which confines rights and injuries, to particular complexions; such the effect of that self-love which justifies, or condemns, not according to principle, but to the agent. Had we turned our eyes inwardly when we supplicated the Father of Mercies to aid the injured and oppressed; when we invoked the Author of Righteousness to attest the purity of our motives, and the justice of our cause;[2] and implored the God of Battles to aid our exertions in its defence, should we not have stood more self convicted than the contrite publican! Should we not have left our gift upon the altar, that we might be first reconciled to our brethren whom we held in bondage? Should we not have loosed their chains, and broken their fetters? Or if the difficulties and dangers of such an experiment prohibited the attempt during the convulsions of a revolution, is it not our duty to embrace the first moment of constitutional health and vigour, to effectuate so desirable an object, and to remove from us a stigma, with which our enemies will never fail to upbraid us, nor our consciences to reproach us? To form a just estimate of this obligation, to demonstrate the incompatibility of a state of slavery with the principles of our government, and of that revolution upon which it is founded, and to elucidate the practicability of its total, though gradual, abolition, it will be proper to consider the nature of slavery, its properties, attendants, and consequences in general; its rise, progress, and present state not only in this commonwealth, but in such of our sister states as have either perfected, or commenced the great work of its extirpation; with the means they have adopted to effect it, and those which the circumstances and situation of our country may render it most expedient for us to pursue, for the attainment of the same noble and important end.[3]

According to Justinian; [1] Lib. 1. Tit. 2. the first general division of persons, in respect to their rights, is into freemen and slaves. It is equally the glory and the happiness of that country from which the citizens of the United States derive their origin, that the traces of slavery, such as at present exists in several of the United States, are there utterly extinguished. It is not my design to enter into a minute enquiry whether it ever had existence there, nor to compare the situation of villeins, during the existence of pure villenage, with that of modern domestic slaves. The records of those times, at least, such as have reached this quarter of the globe, are too few to throw a satisfactory light on the subject. Suffice it that our ancestors migrating hither brought not with them any prototype of that slavery which hath been established among us. The first introduction of it into Virginia was by the arrival of a Dutch ship from the coast of Africa having *twenty* Negroes on board, who were sold here in the year 1620. (2) 2 Stith 182. In the year 1638 we find them in Massachusetts.[4] They were introduced into Connecticut soon after the settlement of that colony; that is to say, about the same period.[5] Thus early had our forefathers sown the seeds of an evil, which, like a leprosy, hath descended upon their posterity with accumulated rancour, visiting the sins of the fathers upon succeeding generations.—The climate of the northern states less favourable to the constitution of the natives of Africa, (3) 3 Dr. Belknap. Zephan. Swift. than the southern, proved alike unfavourable to their propagation, and to the increase of their numbers by importations. As the southern colonies advanced in population, not only importations increased there, but Nature herself, under a climate more congenial to the African constitution, assisted in multiplying the blacks in those parts, no less than in diminishing their numbers in the more rigorous climates of the north; this influence of climate moreover contributed extremely to increase or diminish the value of the slave to the purchasers, in the different colonies. White labourers, whose constitutions were better adapted to the severe winters of the New England colonies, were there found to be preferable to the Negroes, (4) 4 Dr. Belknap. Zephan. Swift. who, accustomed to the influence of an ardent sun, became almost torpid in those countries, not less adapted to give vigour to their laborious exercises, than unfavourable to the multiplication of their species; in those colonies, where the winters were not only milder, and of shorter duration, but succeeded by an intense summer heat, as invigorating to the African, as debilitating to the European constitution, the Negroes were not barely more capable of performing labour than the Europeans, or their descendants, but the multiplication of the species was at least equal; and, where they met with humane treatment, perhaps greater than among the whites. The purchaser therefore calculated not upon the value of the labour of his slave only, but, if a female, he regarded her as "the fruitful mother of an hundred more:" and many of these unfortunate people have there been in this state, whose descendants even in the compass of two or three generations have gone near to realize the calculation.—The great increase of slavery in the southern, in proportion to the northern states in the union, is therefore not attributable, *solely*, to the effect of sentiment, but to natural causes; as well as those considerations of profit, which have, perhaps, an equal influence over the conduct of mankind in general, in whatever country, or under whatever climate their destiny hath placed them. What else but considerations of this nature could have influenced the merchants of the freest nation, at that time in the world, to embark in so nefarious a traffic, as that of the human race, attended, as the African slave trade has been, with the most atrocious aggravations of cruelty, perfidy, and intrigues, the objects of which have been the perpetual fomentation of predatory and intestine wars? What, but similar considerations, could prevail on the government of the same country, even in these days, to patronize a commerce so diametrically opposite to the generally received maxims of that government. It is to the operation of these considerations in the parent country, not less than to their influence in the colonies, that the rise, increase, and continuance of slavery in those British colonies which now constitute united America, are to be attributed, as I shall endeavour to shew in the course of the present enquiry. It is now time to enquire into the nature of slavery, in general, and take a view of its consequences, and attendants in this commonwealth, in particular.

3

Slavery, says a well informed writer [5] 5 Hargrave's case of Negroe Somerset. on the subject, has been attended with circumstances so various in different countries, as to render it difficult to give a general definition of it. Justinian calls it a constitution of the law of nations, by which one man is made subject to another, contrary to nature. [6] 6 Lib. 1. Tit. 3. Sect. 2. Grotius describes it to be an obligation to serve another for life, in consideration of diet, and other common necessaries. [7] 7 Lib. 2. c. 5. Sect. 27 Dr. Rutherforth, rejecting this definition, informs us, that perfect slavery is an obligation to be directed by another in all one's actions. [8] 8 Lib. 1. c. 20. pa. 474. Baron Montesquieu defines it to be the establishment of a right, which gives one man such a power over another, as renders him absolute master over his life and fortune. [9] 9 Lib. 15. c. 1. These definitions appear not to embrace the subject fully, since they respect the condition of the slave, in regard to his *master*, only, and not in regard to the *state*, as well as the *master*. The author last mentioned observes, that the constitution of a state may be free, and the subject not so. The subject free, and not the constitution of the state. [10] 10 Lib. 12. c. 1. Pursuing this idea, instead of attempting a general definition of slavery; I shall, by considering it under a threefold aspect, endeavour to give a just idea of its nature.

I. When a nation is, from any external cause, deprived of the right of being governed by its own laws, only, such a nation may be considered as in a state of *political slavery*. Such is the state of conquered countries, and generally, of colonies, and other dependant governments. Such was the state of united America before the revolution. In this case the personal rights of the subject may be so far secured by wholesome laws, as that the individual may be esteemed free, whilst the state is subject to a higher power: this subjection of one nation, or people, to the will of another, constitutes the first species of slavery, which, in order to distinguish it from the other two, I have called political; inasmuch as it exists only in respect to the governments, and not to the individuals of the two countries. Of this it is not our business to speak, at present.

II. Civil liberty being, no other than natural liberty so far restrained by human laws, and no farther, as is necessary and expedient for the general advantage of the public, [11] 11 Blackstone's Com. c. 125 whenever that liberty is, by the laws of the state, further restrained than is necessary and expedient for the general advantage, a state of *civil slavery* commences immediately: this may affect the whole society, and every description of persons in it, and yet the constitution of the state be perfectly free. And this happens whenever the laws of a state respect the form, or energy of the government, more than the happiness of the citizen; as in Venice, where the most oppressive species of civil slavery exists, extending to every individual in the state, from the poorest gondolier to the members of the senate, and the doge himself.

This species of slavery also exists whenever there is an inequality of rights, or privileges, between the subjects or citizens of the same state, except such as necessarily result from the exercise of a public office; for the pre-eminence of one class of men must be founded and erected upon the depression of another; and the measure of exaltation in the former, is that of the slavery of the latter. In all governments, however constituted, or by what description soever denominated, wherever the distinction of rank prevails, or is admitted by the constitution, this species of slavery exists. It existed in every nation, and in every government in Europe before the French revolution. It existed in the American colonies before they became independent states; and notwithstanding the maxims of equality which have been adopted in their several constitutions, it exists in most, if not all,

4

of them, at this day, in the persons of our free Negroes and mulattoes; whose civil incapacities are almost as numerous as the civil rights of our free citizens. A brief enumeration of them, may not be improper before we proceed to the third head.

Free Negroes and mulattoes are by our constitution excluded from the right of suffrage,[6] and by consequence, I apprehend, from office too: they were formerly incapable of serving in the militia, except as drummers or pioneers, but now I presume they are enrolled in the lists of those that bear arms, though formerly punishable for presuming to appear at a muster-field. (12) 12 1723. c. 2. During the revolution war many of them were enlisted as soldiers in the regular army. Even slaves were not rejected from military service at that period, and such as served faithfully during the period of their enlistment, were emancipated by an act passed after the conclusion of the war. (13) 13 Oct. 1783. c. 3. An act of justice to which they were entitled upon every principle. All but housekeepers, and persons residing upon the frontiers are prohibited from keeping, or carrying any gun, powder, shot, club, or other weapon offensive or defensive: (14) 14 1748. c. 31. Edit. 1794. Resistance to a white person, in any case, was, formerly, and now, in any case, except a wanton assault on the Negroe or mulattoe, is punishable by whipping. (15) 15 Ib. c. 103. No Negroe or mulattoe can be a witness in any prosecution, or civil suit in which a white person is a party. (16) 16 1794. c. 141. Free Negroes together with slaves were formerly denied the benefit of clergy in cases where it was allowed to white persons; but they are now upon an equal footing as to the allowance of clergy, though not as to the consequence of that allowance, inasmuch as the court may superadd other corporal punishments to the burning in the hand usually inflicted upon white persons, in the like cases. (17) 17 1794. c. 103. Emancipated Negroes may be sold to pay the debts of their former master contracted before their emancipation; and they may be hired out to satisfy their taxes where no sufficient distress can be had. Their children are to be bound out apprentices by the overseers of the poor. Free Negroes have all the advantages in capital cases, which white men are entitled to, except a trial by a jury of their own complexion: and a slave suing for his freedom shall have the same privilege. Free Negroes residing, or employed to labour in any town must be registered; the same thing is required of such as go at large in any county. The penalty in both cases is a fine upon the person employing, or harbouring them, and imprisonment of the Negroe. (18) 18 1794. c. 163. The migration of free Negroes or mulattoes to this state is also prohibited; and those who do migrate hither may be sent back to the place from whence they came. (19) 19 1794. c. 164. Any person, not being a Negroe, having one-fourth or more Negroe blood in him is deemed a mulattoe. The law makes no other distinction between Negroes and mulattoes, whether slaves or freemen. These incapacities and disabilities are evidently the fruit of the third species of slavery, of which it remains to speak; or, rather, they are scions from the same common stock: which is,

III. That condition in which one man is subject to be directed by another in all his actions; and this constitutes a state of *domestic slavery*; to which state all the incapacities and disabilities of civil slavery are incident, with the weight of other numerous calamities superadded thereto. And here it may be proper to make a short enquiry into the origin and foundation of domestic slavery in other countries, previous to its fatal introduction into this.

5

Slaves, says Justinian, are either born such or become so. [20] 20 Inst. lib. 1. tit. 1. They are born slaves when they are children of bond women; and they become slaves, either by the law of nations, that is, by captivity; for it is the practice of our generals to sell their captives, being accustomed to preserve, and not to destroy them: or by the civil law, which happens when a free person, above the age of twenty, suffers himself to be sold for the sake of sharing the price given for him. The author of the Commentaries on the Laws of England thus combats the reasonableness of all these grounds: [21] 21 1. b. c. 423. "The conqueror," says he, "according to the civilians, had a right to the life of his captives; and having spared that, has a right to deal with him as he pleases. But it is an untrue position, when taken generally, that by the law of nature or nations, a man may kill his enemy: he has a right to kill him only in particular cases; in cases of absolute necessity for self-defence; and it is plain that this absolute necessity did not subsist, since the victor did not actually kill him, but made him prisoner. War itself is justifiable only on principles of self-preservation; and therefore it gives no other right over prisoners but merely to disable them from doing harm to us, by confining their persons: much less can it give a right to kill, torture, abuse, plunder, or even to enslave, an enemy, when the war is over. Since therefore the right of *making* slaves by captivity, depends on a supposed right of slaughter, that foundation failing, the consequence drawn from it must fail likewise. But, secondly, it is said slavery may begin *jure civili*; when one man sells himself to another. This, if only meant of contracts to serve, or work for, another, is very just: but when applied to strict slavery, in the sense of the laws of old Rome or modern Barbary, is also impossible. Every sale implies a price, a *quid pro quo*, an equivalent given to the seller, in lieu of what he transfers to the buyer; but what equivalent can be given for life and liberty, both of which, in absolute slavery, are held to be in the master's disposal? His property, also, the very price he seems to receive, devolves, *ipso facto*, to his master, the instant he becomes a slave. In this case, therefore, the buyer gives nothing, and the seller receives nothing: of what validity then can a sale be, which destroys the very principles upon which all sales are founded? Lastly we are told, that besides these two ways by which slaves are acquired, they may also be hereditary; "*servi nascuntur*;" the children of acquired slaves are, "jure naturæ," by a negative kind of birthright, slaves also.—But *this, being built on the two former rights*, must *fall* together with them. If neither captivity, nor the sale of one's self, can by the law of nature and reason reduce the parent to slavery, *much less* can they reduce the offspring." Thus by the most clear, manly, and convincing reasoning does this excellent author refute every claim upon which the practice of slavery is founded, or by which it has been supposed to be justified, at least, in modern times.[7] But were we even to admit, that a captive taken in a *just war*, might by his conqueror be reduced to a state of slavery, this could not justify the claim of Europeans to reduce the natives of Africa to that state: it is a melancholy, though well-known fact, that in order to furnish supplies of these unhappy people for the purposes of the slave trade, the Europeans have constantly, by the most insidious (I had almost said infernal) arts, fomented a kind of perpetual warfare among the ignorant and miserable people of Africa; and instances have not been wanting, where, by the most shameful breach of faith, they have trepanned and made slaves of the *sellers* as well as the *sold*.[8] That such horrid practices have been sanctioned by a civilized nation; that a nation ardent in the cause of liberty, and enjoying its blessings in the fullest extent, can continue to vindicate a right established upon such a foundation; that a people who have declared, "That *all men* are by nature *equally* [22] 22 Bill of Rights, art. 1. *free* and *independent*," and have made this declaration the first article in the foundation of their government, should in defiance of so sacred a truth, recognized by

6

themselves in so solemn a manner, and on so important an occasion, tolerate a practice incompatible therewith, is such an evidence of the weakness and inconsistency of human nature, as every man who hath a spark of patriotic fire in his bosom must wish to see removed from his own country. If ever there was a cause, if ever an occasion, in which all hearts should be united, every nerve strained, and every power exerted, surely the restoration of human nature to its inalienable right is such: Whatever obstacles, therefore, may hitherto have retarded the attempt, he that can appreciate the honour and happiness of his country, will think it time that we should attempt to surmount them.

But how loudly soever reason, justice, and (may I not add) religion,[9] condemn the practice of slavery, it is acknowledged to have been very ancient, and almost universal. The Greeks, the Romans, and the ancient Germans also practiced it, as well as the more ancient Jews and Egyptians. By the Germans it was transmitted to the various kingdoms which arose in Europe out of the ruins of the Roman empire. In England it subsisted for some ages under the name of *villeinage*.[10] In Asia it seems to have been general, and in Africa universal, and so remains to this day: In Europe it hath long since declined; its first declension there, is said to have been in Spain, as early as the eighth century; and it is alleged to have been general about the middle of the fourteenth, and was near expiring in the sixteenth, when the discovery of the American continent, and the eastern and western coasts of Africa gave rise to the introduction of a new species of slavery. It took its origin from the Portuguese, who, in order to supply the Spaniards with persons able to sustain the fatigue of cultivating their new possessions in America, particularly the islands, opened a trade between Africa and America for the sale of Negroes, about the year 1508. The expedient of having slaves for labour was not long peculiar to the Spaniards, being afterwards adopted by other European colonies: (23) 23 Hargrave, ib. and though some attempts have been made to stop its progress in most of the United States, and several of them have the fairest prospects of success in attempting the extirpation of it, yet is others, it hath taken such deep root, as to require the most strenuous exertions to eradicate it.

The first introduction of Negroes into Virginia happened, as we have already mentioned, in the year 1620; from that period to the year 1662 there is no compilation of our laws, in print, now to be met with. In the revision made in that year, we find an act declaring that no Englishman, trader, or other, who shall bring in any Indians as servants and assign them over to any other, shall sell them for *slaves*, nor for any other time than English of like age should serve by act of assembly. (24) 24 1662. c. 136. The succeeding session all children born in this country were declared to be bond, or free, according to the condition of the mother. (25) 25 1662. Sess. d. c. 12. In 1667 it was declared, "That the conferring of baptism doth not alter the condition of the person baptized, as to his bondage or freedom." (26) 26 1667. c. 2. This was done, "that divers masters freed from this doubt may more carefully endeavour the propagating of Christianity, by permitting their slaves to be baptized." It would have been happy for this unfortunate race of men if the same tender regard for their bodies, had always manifested itself in our laws, as is shewn for their souls in this act. But this was not the case; for two years after, we meet with an act, declaring, "That if any slave resist his master, or others, by his master's orders correcting him, and by the extremity of the correction should chance to die, such death should not be accounted felony: but the master or other person appointed by his master to punish him, be acquit from molestation: *since it could not be presumed that prepensive malice*, which alone makes *murder felony*, should induce any man to destroy his own estate."[11] This cruel and tyrannical act was, at three different periods (27) 27 1705. c. 49.

7

1723. c. 4. 1748. c. 31. re-enacted, with very little alteration; and was not finally repealed till the year 1788 (28) 28 1788. c. 23.—above a century after it had first disgraced our code. In 1668 we meet with the first traces of emancipation, in an act which subjects Negroe women set free to the tax on titheables. (29) 29 1668. c. 7. Two years after, (30) 30 1670. c. 5. an act passed prohibiting *Indians* or Negroes, manumitted, or otherwise set free, though baptized, from purchasing Christian servants. (31) 31 1670. c. 12. From this act it is evident that*Indians* had *before* that time been made slaves, as well as Negroes, though we have no traces of the original act by which they were reduced to that condition. An act of the same session recites that disputes had arisen whether Indians taken in war by any other nation, and by that nation sold to the English, are servants for *life*, or for a term of years; and declaring that all *servants*, not being Christians, imported into this country by *shipping*, shall be *slaves* for their life-time; but that what shall come by land, shall serve, if boys and girls, until thirty years of age; if men and women twelve years, and no longer. On a rupture with the Indians in the year 1679 it was, for the*better encouragement of soldiers*, declared that what *Indian* prisoners should be*taken in war* should be free purchase to the soldier *taking* them. (32) 32 1679. c. 1. Three years after it was declared that all *servants* brought into this country by sea or land, not being Christians, whether Negroes, Moors, mulattoes or Indians, except Turks and Moors in amity with Great Britain, and all Indians which should thereafter be sold by neighbouring Indians, or any others trafficking with us, as slaves, should be slaves to all intents and purposes. (33) 33 1682. c. 1. This act was re-enacted in the year 1705, and afterwards in 1753, (34) 34 1705 c. 49. 1753. c. 2. nearly in the same terms. In 1705 an act was made, authorising a free and open trade for all persons, at all times, and at all places, with all Indians whatsoever. (35) 35 1705 c. 52. On the authority of this act, the general court in April term 1787 decided that no Indians brought into Virginia since the passing thereof, nor their descendants, can be slaves in this commonwealth.[12] In October 1778 the general assembly passed the first act which occurs in our code for prohibiting the importation of slaves; (36) 36 1778. c. 1. thereby declaring that no slave should thereafter be brought into this commonwealth by land, or by water; and that every slave imported contrary thereto, should upon such importation be free: with an exception as to such as might belong to persons migrating from the other states, or be claimed by descent, devise, or marriage, or be at that time the actual property of any citizen of this commonwealth, residing in any other of the United States, or belonging to travellers making a transient stay, and carrying their slaves away with them.—In 1705 this act unfortunately underwent some alteration, by declaring that slaves thereafter brought into this commonwealth, and kept therein one whole *year together*, or so long at different times as shall *amount to a year*, shall be free. By this means the difficulty of proving the right to freedom will be not a little augmented: for the fact of the first importation, where the right to freedom immediately ensued, might have been always proved without difficulty; but where a slave is subject to removal from place to place, and his right to freedom is postponed for so long a time as a whole year, or perhaps several years, the provisions in favour of liberty may be too easily evaded. The same act declares that no persons shall thenceforth be slaves in this commonwealth, except such as were so on the first day of that session (Oct. 17th, 1785), and the descendants of the females of them. This act was re-enacted in the revisal made in 1792. (37) 37 See acts of 1794, c. 103. In 1793 an additional act passed, authorising and requiring any justice of the peace having notice of the importation of any slaves, directly or indirectly, from any part of Africa or the West Indies, to cause such slave to be immediately apprehended and transported out of the commonwealth. (38) 38 Edit. of 1794. c. 164. Such is the rise, progress, and present foundation of slavery in Virginia, so far as I have been able to trace it. The present number of slaves in Virginia, is immense, as appears by the census taken in 1791, amounting to no less than 292,427 souls: nearly two-fifths of the whole population of the commonwealth.[13] We may console ourselves with the hope that this proportion will not increase, the further importation of slaves being prohibited, whilst the free migrations of white people hither is encouraged. But this hope affords no other relief from the evil of slavery, than a diminution of those apprehensions which are naturally excited by the detention of so large a number of oppressed individuals among us, and the possibility that they may one day be roused to an attempt to shake off their chains.

Whatever inclination the first inhabitants of Virginia might have to encourage slavery, a disposition to check its progress, and increase, manifested itself in the legislature even before the close of the last century. So long ago as the year 1669 we find the title of an act, (39) 39 Edit. of 1733. c. 12. laying an imposition upon *servants*, and *slaves*, imported into this country; which was either continued, revised, or increased, by a variety of temporary acts, passed between that period and the revolution in 1776.[14]—One of these acts passed in 1723, by a marginal note appears to have been repealed by proclamation, Oct. 24, 1724. In 1732 a duty of five per cent. was laid on slaves imported, to be paid by the buyers; a measure calculated to render it as little obnoxious as possible to the *English* merchants trading to Africa, and not improbably suggested by them, to the privy council in England. The preamble to this act is in these remarkable words, "We your majesty's most dutiful and loyal subjects, &c. taking into our serious consideration the exigencies of your government here, and that the duty laid upon liquors will not be sufficient to defray the necessary expences thereof, do humbly represent to your majesty, that *no other* duty can be laid upon our import or export, without oppressing your subjects, than a duty upon *slaves imported*, to be paid by the buyers, *agreeable to your majesty's instructions* to your lieutenant governor." This act was only for the short period of four years, but seems to have been continued from time to time till the year 1751, when the duty expired, but was revived the next year. In the year 1740 an additional duty of five per cent. was imposed for four years, for the purpose of an expedition against the Spaniards, &c. to be likewise paid by the buyers: and in 1742 the whole duty was continued till July 1, 1747.—The act of 1752, by which these duties were revived and continued (as well as several former acts), takes notice that the duty had been found *no ways burdensome to the traders* in slaves. In 1754 an additional duty of five per cent. was imposed for the term of three years, by an act for encouraging and protecting the settlers on the Missisippi: this duty, like all the former, was to be paid by the buyers. In 1759 a duty of 20 per cent. was imposed upon all slaves imported into Virginia from Maryland, North Carolina, or other places in America, to continue for seven years. In 1769 the same duty was further continued. In the same session the duty of five per cent. was continued for three years, and an additional duty of ten per cent. to be likewise paid by the buyers, was imposed for seven years; and a further duty of five per cent. was, by a separate act of the same session, imposed for the better support of the contingent charges of government, to be paid by the buyers. In 1772 all these duties were further continued for the term of five years from the expiration of the acts then in force: the assembly at the same time petitioned the throne,[15] *to remove all those restraints which inhibited* his majesty's governors assenting to such *laws* as *might check so very pernicious a commerce*, as that of slavery.

In the course of this enquiry it is easy to trace the desire of the legislature to put a stop to the further importation of slaves; and had not this desire been uniformly opposed on the part of the crown, it is highly probable that event would have taken effect at a much earlier period than it did. A duty of five per cent. to be paid by the buyers, at first, with difficulty obtained the royal assent. Requisitions from the crown for aids, on particular occasions, afforded a pretext from time to time for increasing the duty from five, to ten, and finally to twenty per cent. with which the *buyer* was uniformly made chargeable. The wishes of the people of this colony, were not sufficient to counterbalance the interest of the English merchants, trading to Africa, and it is probable, that however disposed to put a stop to so infamous a traffic by law, we should never have been able to effect it, so long as we might have continued dependant on the British government: an object sufficient of itself to justify a revolution. That the legislature of Virginia were *sincerely* disposed to put a stop to it, cannot be doubted; for even during the tumult and confusion of the revolution, we have seen that they availed themselves of the earliest opportunity, to crush for ever so pernicious and infamous a commerce, by an act passed in October 1778, the penalties of which, though apparently lessened by the act of 1792, are still equal to the value of the slave; being two hundred dollars upon the importer, and one hundred dollars upon every person buying or selling an imported slave.

A system uniformly persisted in for nearly a whole century, and finally carried into effect, so soon as the legislature was unrestrained by "the inhuman exercise of the royal negative," evinces the sincerity of that disposition which the legislature had shewn during so long a period, to put a check to the growing evil. From the time that the duty was raised above five per cent. it is probable that the importation of slaves into this colony decreased. The demand for them in the more southern colonies probably contributed also to lessen the numbers imported into this: for some years immediately preceding the revolution, the importation of slaves into Virginia might almost be considered as at an end; and probably would have been entirely so, if the ingenuity of the merchant had not found out the means of evading the heavy duty, by pretended sales, at which the slaves were bought in by some friend, at a quarter of their real value.

Tedious and unentertaining as this detail may appear to all others, a citizen of Virginia will feel some satisfaction at reading so clear a vindication of his country, from the opprobrium, but too lavishly bestowed upon her of fostering slavery in her bosom, whilst she boasts a sacred regard to the liberty of her citizens, and of mankind in general. The acrimony of such censures must abate, at least in the breasts of the candid, upon an impartial review of the subject here brought before them; and if in addition to what we have already advanced, they consider the difficulties attendant on any plan for the abolition of slavery, in a country where so large a proportion of the inhabitants are slaves; and where a still larger proportion of the cultivators of the earth are of that description of men, they will probably feel emotions of sympathy and compassion, both for the slave and for his master, succeed to those hasty prejudices, which even the best dispositions are not exempt from contracting, upon subjects where there is a deficiency of information.

We are next to consider the condition of slaves in Virginia, or the legal consequences attendant on a state of slavery in this commonwealth; and here it is not my intention to notice those laws, which consider slaves, merely as *property*, and have from time to time been enacted to regulate the disposition of them, *as such*; for these will be more properly considered elsewhere: my intention at present is therefore to take a view of such laws, only, as regard slaves, as a distinct class of *persons*, whose rights, if indeed they possess any, are reduced to a much narrower compass, than those, of which we have been speaking before.

Civil rights, we may remember, are reducible to three primary heads; the right of personal security; the right of personal liberty; and the right of private property. In a state of slavery the two last are wholly abolished, the person of the slave being at the absolute disposal of his master; and property, what he is incapable, in that state, either of acquiring, or holding, to his own use. Hence it will appear how perfectly irreconcilable a state of slavery is to the principles of a democracy, which form the *basis* and *foundation* of our government. For our bill of rights declares, "that all men are by nature *equally free* and independent, and have certain rights of which they cannot deprive or divest their posterity—namely, *the enjoyment of life and *liberty*, with the means of *acquiring* and *possessing property*." This is indeed no more than a recognition of the first principles of the law of nature, which teaches us this equality, and enjoins every man, whatever advantages he may possess over another, as to the various qualities or endowments of body or mind, to practice the precepts of the law of nature to those who are in these respects his *inferiors*, no less than it enjoins his *inferiors* to practise them towards *him*. Since he has no more right to insult *them*, than they have to injure him. Nor does the *bare unkindness of nature* or of fortune condemn a man to a *worse* condition than others, as to the enjoyment of common privileges. (40) 40 Spavan's Puff. vol. 1. c. 17. It would be hard to reconcile reducing the Negroes to a state of slavery to these principles, unless we first degrade them below the rank of human beings, not only politically, but also physically and morally.—The Roman lawyers look upon those only properly as *persons*, who are *free*, putting *slaves* into the rank of *goods* and *chattels*; and the policy of our legislature, as well as the practice of slave-holders in America in general, seems conformable to that idea: but surely it is time we should admit the evidence of moral truth, and learn to regard them as our fellow men, and equals, except in those particulars where accident, or perhaps nature, may have give us some advantage; a recompence for which they perhaps enjoy in other respects.

Slavery, says Hargrave, always imports an obligation of perpetual service, which only the consent of the master can dissolve: it also generally gives to the master an arbitrary power of administring every sort of correction, however inhuman, not immediately affecting life or limb, and even these in some countries, as formerly in Rome, and at this day among the Asiatics and Africans, are left exposed to the arbitrary will of a master, or protected only by fines or other slight punishments. The property of the slave also is absolutely the property of his master, the slave himself being the subject of property, and as such saleable, or transmissible at the will of his master.—A slavery, so malignant as that described, does not leave to its wretched victims the least vestige of any civil right, and even divests them of all their natural rights. It does not, however, appear, that the rigours of slavery in this country were ever as great, as those above described: yet it must be confessed, that, at times, they have fallen very little short of them.

The first severe law respecting slaves, now to be met with in our code, is that of 1669, already mentioned, which declared that the death of a slave *resisting* his master, or other person correcting him by his order, *happening by extremity of the correction*, should not be accounted felony. The alterations which this law underwent in three successive acts, (41) 41 1705. c. 49. 1723, c. 4. 1748. c. 31. were by no means calculated effectually to mitigate its severity; it seems rather to have been augmented by the act of 1723, which declared that a person indicted for the murder of a slave, and found guilty of *manslaughter*, should not incur any punishment for the same.[16]

All these acts were at length repealed in 1788. (42) 42 1788. 2. 23. So that homicide of a slave stands now upon the same footing, as in the case of any other person. In 1672 it

11

was declared lawful for any person pursuing any runaway Negroe, mulattoe, Indian slave, or *servant for life*, by virtue of an *hue and cry*, to kill them in case of resistance, without being questioned for the same. [43] [43 1672. c. 8.] A few years afterwards this act was extended to persons *employed to apprehend* runaways. [44] [44 1680. c. 10.] In 1705, these acts underwent some small alteration; two justices being authorised by proclamation to *outlaw* runaways, who might thereafter be *killed* and destroyed by any person whatsoever, by *such ways and means* as he may think fit, without accusation or impeachment of any crime for so doing: [45] [45 1705. c. 49.] And if any such slave were apprehended, he might be punished at the discretion of the county court, either by *dismembering*, or in any other manner not *touching life*. The inhuman rigour of this act was afterwards [46] [46 1723. c. 4. 1748. c. 31.] extended to the venial offence of going abroad by night, if the slave was *notoriously* guilty of it.—Such are the cruelties to which a state of slavery gives birth; such the horrors to which the human mind is capable of being reconciled, by its adoption. The dawn of humanity at length appeared in the year 1769, when the power of dismembering, even under the authority of a county court, was restricted to the single offence of *attempting* to ravish a white woman, [47] [47 1769. c. 19.] in which case perhaps the punishment is perhaps not more than commensurate to the crime. In 1772 some restraints were laid upon the practice of outlawing slaves, requiring that it should appear to the *satisfaction* of the justices that the slaves were outlying, and *doing mischief*. [48] [48 1772. c. 9.] These loose expressions of the act, left too much in the discretion of men, not much addicted to weighing their import.—In 1792, every thing relative to the outlawry of slaves was *expunged* from our code, [49] [49 Edit. 1794. c. 103.] and I trust will never again find a place in it. By the act of 1680, a Negroe, mulattoe, or Indian, bond or *free*, presuming to lift his hand in opposition to any Christian, should receive thirty lashes on his bare back for every offence. [50] [50 1680. c. 10. 1705. c.] The same act prohibited slaves from carrying any club, staff, gun, sword, or other weapon, offensive or defensive. This was afterwards extended to all Negroes, mulattoes and Indians whatsoever, with a few exceptions in favour of housekeepers, residents on a frontier plantation, and such as were enlisted in the militia. [51] [51 1723. c. 4.] Slaves, by these and other acts, [52] [52 1705. c. 49. 1723. c. 4. 1748. c. 31. 1753. c. 2. 1785. c. 77.] are prohibited from going abroad without leave in writing from their masters, and if they do, may be whipped: any person suffering a slave to remain on his plantation for four hours together, or dealing with him without leave in writing from his master, is subject to a fine. A runaway slave may be apprehended and committed to jail, and if not claimed within three months (being first advertised) he shall be hired out, having an iron collar first put about his neck: and if not claimed within a year shall be sold. [53] [53 1753. c. 2.] These provisions were in general re-enacted in 1792, [54] [54 Edit. of 1794. c. 103. 131.] but the punishment to be inflicted on a Negroe or mulattoe, for lifting his hand against a white person, is restricted to those cases, where the former is not wantonly assaulted. In this act the word Indian appears to have been designedly omitted: the small number of these people, or their descendants remaining among us, concurring with a more liberal way of thinking, probably gave occasion to this circumstance. The act of 1748, c. 31, made it felony without benefit of clergy for a slave to prepare, exhibit, or administer any medicine whatever, without the order or consent of the master; but *allowed clergy* if it appeared that the medicine was not administered with an *ill intent*; the act of 1792, with more justice, directs that in such case he shall be acquitted. [55] 55 Edit. 1794. c. 103. To consult, advise, or conspire, to rebel, or to plot, or conspire the death of any person whatsoever, is still felony without benefit of clergy in a slave. [56] 56 1748. c. 31. 1794. c. 103.—Riots, routs, unlawful assemblies, trespasses and seditious speeches by slaves, are punishable with stripes, at the discretion of a justice of the peace. [57] 57 1785. c. 77. 1794. c. 103.—The master of a slave permitting him to go at large and trade as a freeman, is subject to a fine; [58] 58 1769. c. 19. May 1782. c. 32. 1794. Ib. and if she suffers the slave to hire himself out, the latter may be sold, and twenty-five per cent. of the price be applied to the use of the county.—Negroes and mulattoes, whether slaves or not, are incapable of being witnesses, but against, or between Negroes and mulattoes; they are not permitted to intermarry with any white person; yet no punishment is annexed to the offence in the slave; nor is the marriage void; but the white person contracting the marriage, and the clergyman by whom it is celebrated are liable to fine and imprisonment; and this is probably the only instance in which our laws will be found more favourable to a Negroe than a white person. These provisions though introduced into our code at different periods, were all re-enacted in 1792. [59] 59 Edit. of 1794. c. 103.

From this melancholy review it will appear that not only the right of property, and the right of personal liberty, but even the right of personal security, has been, at times, either wholly annihilated, or reduced to a shadow: and even in these days, the protection of the latter seems to be confined to very few cases. Many actions, indifferent in themselves, being permitted by the law of nature to all mankind, and by the laws of society to all free persons, are either rendered highly criminal in a slave, or subject him to some kind of punishment or restraint. Nor is it in this respect only, that his condition is rendered thus deplorable by law. The measure of punishment for the same offence, is often, and the manner of trial and conviction is always, different in the case of a slave, and a free-man. If the latter be accused of any crime, he is entitled to an examination before the court of the county where the offence is alleged to have been committed; whose decision, if in his favour, is held to be a legal and final acquittal, but it is not final if against him; for after this, both a grand jury, and a petit jury of the county, must successively pronounce him guilty; the former by the concurrent voices of twelve at least, of their body, and the latter, by their unanimous verdict upon oath. He may take exception to the proceedings against him, by a motion in arrest of judgment; and in this case, or if there be a special verdict, the same unanimity between his judges, as between his jurors, is necessary to his condemnation. Lastly, through the punishment which the law pronounces for his offence amount to death itself, he shall in many cases have the benefit of clergy, unless he has before received it. But in the case of a slave, the mode was formerly, and still remains essentially different. How early this distinction was adopted I have not been able to discover. The title of an act occurs, which passed in the year 1705 [60] 60 1705. c. 11. for the *speedy* and *easy* prosecution of slaves committing capital crimes. In 1723 [61] 61 1723. c. 4. the governor was authorized, whenever any slave was committed for any capital offence, to issue a special commission of oyer and terminer, to *such persons as he should think fit*, the number being left to his discretion, who should thereupon proceed to the trial of such slave, taking for evidence the confession of the defendant, the oath of one or more credible witnesses, or such testimony of Negroes, mulattoes, or Indians, bond or free, with pregnant circumstances, as to them should seem convincing, without the solemnity of a jury. No exception, formerly, could be taken to the

13

proceedings, on the trial of a slave, (62) 62 1748. c. 31. but that proviso is omitted in the act of 1792, and the justices moreover seem bound to allow him counsel for his defence, whose fee shall be paid by his master (63) 63 Edit. 1794. c. 103. In case of conviction, execution of the sentence was probably very speedily performed, since the act of 1748, provides that, thereafter, it should not be performed in less than ten days, except in case of insurrection or rebellion; and further, that if the court be divided in opinion the accused should be acquitted. In 1764, an act passed, authorizing general, instead of special, commissioners of oyer and terminer, (64) 64 1764. c. 9. constituting all the justices of any county, judges for the trial of slaves, committing capital offences, within their respective counties; any four of whom, one being of the quorum, should constitute a court for that purpose. In 1772 one step further was made in favour of humanity, by an act declaring that no slave should thereafter be condemned to die unless four of the court should concur in opinion of his guilt. (65) 65 1772. c. 9. The act of 1786, c. 58, confirmed by that of 1792, constitutes the justices of every county and corporation justices of oyer and terminer for the trial of slaves; (66) 66 Edit. 1794. c. 103. requires *five* justices, at least, to constitute a court, and *unanimity* in the court for his condemnation; allows him counsel for his defence, to be paid by his owner, and, I apprehend, admits him to object to the proceedings against him; and finally enlarges the time of execution to *thirty* days, instead of ten (except in cases of conspiracy, insurrection, or rebellion), and extends the benefit of clergy to him in all cases, where any other person should have the benefit thereof, except in the cases before mentioned.

To an attentive observer these gradual, and almost imperceptible amendments in our jurisprudence respecting slaves, will be found, upon the whole, of infinite importance to that unhappy race. The mode of trial in criminal cases, especially, is rendered infinitely more beneficial to them, than formerly, though perhaps still liable to exception for want of the aid of a jury: the solemnity of an oath administered the moment the trial commences, may be considered as operating more forcibly on the mind, than a general oath of office, taken, perhaps, twenty years before. Unanimity may also be more readily expected to take place among *five* men, than among *twelve*. These objections to the want of a jury are not without weight: on the other hand it may be observed, that if the number of triers be not equal to a full jury, they may yet be considered as more select; a circumstance of infinitely greater importance to the slave. The unanimity requisite in the court in order to conviction, is a more happy acquisition to the accused, than may at first appear; the opinions of the court must be delivered openly, immediately, and seriatim, beginning with the youngest judge. A single voice in favour of the accused, is an acquittal; for unanimity is not necessary, as with a jury, to acquit, as well as to condemn: there is less danger in this mode of trial, where the suffrages are to be openly delivered, that a few will be brought over to the opinion of the majority, as may too often happen among jurors, whose deliberations are in *private*, and whose impatience of confinement may go further than real conviction, to produce the requisite unanimity. That this happens not unfrequently in civil cases, there is too much reason to believe; that it may also happen in criminal cases, especially where the party accused is not one of their equals, might, not unreasonably, be apprehended. In New-York, before the revolution, a slave accused of a capital crime, should have been tried by a jury if his master required it. This is, perhaps, still the law of that state. Such a provision might not be amiss in this; but considering the ordinary run of juries in the county-courts, I should presume the privilege would be rarely insisted upon.

Slaves, we have seen, are now entitled to the benefit of clergy in all cases where it is allowed to any other offenders, except in cases of consulting, advising, or conspiring to

14

rebel, or make insurrection; or plotting or conspiring to murder any person; or preparing, exhibiting, or administring medicine with an *ill* intent. The same lenity was not extended to them formerly. The act of 1748, c. 31, denied it to a slave in case of manslaughter; or the felonious breaking and entering *any* house, in the night time: or breaking and entering *any* house in the day time, and taking therefrom goods to the value of twenty shillings. The act of 1764, c. 9, extended the benefit of clergy, to a slave convicted of the manslaughter of a slave; and the act of 1772, c. 9, extended it further, to a slave convicted of housebreaking in the night time, unless such breaking be burglary; in the latter case, other offenders would be equally deprived of it. But wherever the benefit of clergy is allowed to a slave, the court, besides burning him in the hand (the usual punishment inflicted on free persons) may inflict such further corporal punishment as they may think fit; [67] [67] 1794. c. 103. this also seems to be the law in the case of free Negroes and mulattoes. By the act of 1723, c. 4, it was enacted, that when *any Negroe* or *mulattoe* shall be found, upon due proof made, or *pregnant circumstances*, to have given false testimony, every such offender shall, *without further trial*, have his ears successively nailed to the pillory for the space of an hour, and then cut off, and moreover receive thirty-nine lashes on his bare back, or such other punishment as the court shall think proper, not extending to life or limb. This act, with the exception of the words *pregnant circumstances*, was re-enacted in 1792. The punishment of perjury, in a *white* person, is only a fine and imprisonment. A slave convicted of hog-stealing, shall, for the first offence, receive thirty-nine lashes: any other person twenty-five: but the latter is also subject to a fine of thirty dollars, besides paying eight dollars to the owner of the hog. The punishment for the second and third offence, of this kind, is the same in the case of a free person, as of a slave; namely, by the pillory and loss of ears, for the second offence; the third is declared felony, to which clergy is, however, allowed. The preceding are the only positive distinctions which now remain between the punishment of a slave, and a white person, in those cases, where the latter is liable to a determinate corporal punishment. But we must not forget, that many actions, which are either not punishable at all, when perpetrated by a white person, or at most, by fine and imprisonment, only, are liable to severe corporal punishment, when done by a slave; nay, even to death itself, in some cases. To go abroad without a written permission; to keep or carry a gun, or other weapon; to utter any seditious speech; to be present at any unlawful assembly of slaves; to lift the hand in opposition to a white person, unless wantonly assaulted, are all offences punishable by whipping.[68] [68] 1794. c. 103. To attempt the chastity of a white woman, forcibly, is punishable by dismemberment: such an attempt would be a high misdemeanor in a white free man, but the punishment would be far short of that of a slave. [69] [69] Ibidem. To administer medicine without the order or consent of the master, unless it *appear not to have been done with an ill intent*; to *consult*, advise, or conspire, to rebel or make insurrection; or to *conspire*, or *plot* to *murder* any person, we have seen, are all capital offences, from which the benefit of clergy is utterly excluded. But a *bare intention* to commit a felony, is not punishable in the case of a free white man; and even the attempt, if not attended with an actual breach of the peace, or prevented by such circumstance; only, as do not tend to lessen the guilt of the offender, is at most a misdemeanor by the common law: and in statutable offences in general, to consult, advise, and even to procure any person to commit a felony, does not constitute the crime of felony in the adviser or procurer, unless the felony be actually perpetrated.

From this view of our jurisprudence respecting slaves, we are unavoidably led to remark, how frequently the laws of nature have been set aside in favour of institutions, the pure result of prejudice, usurpation, and tyranny. We have found actions, innocent, or indifferent, punishable with a rigour scarcely due to any, but the most atrocious, offences against civil society; justice distributed by an unequal measure to the master and the slave; and even the hand of mercy arrested, where mercy might have been extended to the wretched culprit, had his complexion been the same with that of his judges: for, the short period of ten days, between his condemnation and execution, was often insufficient to obtain a pardon for a slave, convicted in a remote part of the country, whilst a free man, condemned at the seat of government, and tried before the governor himself, in whom the power of pardoning was vested, had a respite of thirty days to implore the clemency of the executive authority.—It may be urged, and I believe with truth, that these rigours do not proceed from a sanguinary temper in the people of Virginia, but from those political considerations indispensibly necessary, where slavery prevails to any great extent: I am moreover happy to observe that our police respecting this unhappy class of people, is not only less rigorous than formerly, but perhaps milder than in any other country[17] where there are so many slaves, or so large a proportion of them, in respect to the free inhabitants: it is also, I trust, unjust to censure the present generation for the existence of slavery in Virginia: for I think it unquestionably true, that a very large proportion of our fellow-citizens lament that as a misfortune, which is imputed to them as a reproach; it being evident from what has been already shewn upon the subject, that, *antecedent to the revolution*, no exertion to abolish, or even to check the progress of, slavery, in Virginia, could have received the smallest countenance from the crown, without whose assent the united wishes and exertions of every individual here, would have been wholly fruitless and ineffectual: it is, perhaps, also demonstrable, that at no period since the revolution, could the abolition of slavery in this state have been safely undertaken until the foundations of our newly established governments had been found capable of supporting the fabric itself, under any shock, which so arduous an attempt might have produced. But these obstacles being now happily removed, considerations of policy, as well as justice and humanity, must evince the necessity of eradicating the evil, before it becomes impossible to do it, without tearing up the roots of civil society with it.

Having in the preceding part of this enquiry shewn the origin and foundation of slavery, or the manner in which men have become slaves, as also who are liable to be retained in slavery, in Virginia, at present, with the legal consequences attendant upon their condition; it only remains to consider the mode by which slaves have been or may be emancipated; and the legal consequences thereof, in this state.—Manumission, among the Israelites, if the bondman were an Hebrew, was enjoined after six years' service, by the Mosaical law, unless the servant chose to continue with his master, in which case the master carried him before the judges, and took an awl, and thrust it through his ear into the door, (70)[70 Exod. c. 21. Deut. c. 15.] and from thenceforth he became a servant for ever: but if he sent him away free, he was bound to furnish him liberally out of his flock, and out of his floor, and out of his wine-press. (71)[71 Ibid.] Among the Romans, in the time of the commonwealth, liberty could be conferred only three ways. By testament, by the *census*, and by the *vindicta*, or lictor's rod. A man was said to be free by the census, "*liber censu*," when his name was inserted in the censor's roll, with the approbation of his master. When he was freed by the vindicta, the master placing his hand upon the head of the slave, said in the presence of the prætor, it is my desire that this man may be free, "*hunc hominem liberem esse volo;*" to which the prætor replied, I pronounce him free after the manner of the Romans, "*dico cum liberum esse more quiritum.*"—then the lictor, receiving the *vindicta*, struck the new freed man several blows with it, upon the head, face, and back, after which his name was registered in the roll of freed-men, and his head being close

16

shaved, a cap was given him as a token of liberty. (72) 72 Harris's Just. in notes. Under the imperial constitutions liberty might have been conferred by several other methods, as in the face of the church, in the presence of friends, or by letter, or by testament. (73) 73 Just. Inst. lib. 1. tit. 5. Ib. lib. 1. tit. 6.—But it was not in the power of every master to manumit at will; for if it were done with an intent to defraud creditors, the act was void; that is, if the master were insolvent at the time of manumission, or became insolvent by manumission, and intentionally manumitted his slave for the purpose of defrauding his creditors. A minor, under the age of twenty years, could not manumit his slave but for a just cause assigned, which must have been approved by a council, consisting of the prætor, five senators, and five knights. (74) 74 Ib. Harris's Just. in notes.—In England, the mode of enfranchising villeins is said to have been thus prescribed by a law of William the Conqueror. "If any person is willing to enfranchise his *slave*, let him, with his right hand, deliver the slave to the sheriff in a full county, proclaim him exempt from the bond of servitude by manumission, shew him open gates and ways, and deliver him *free arms*, to wit, a lance and a sword; thereupon he is a free man." (75) 75 Harris's Inst. in notes.—But after that period freedom was more generally conferred by deed, of which Mr. Harris, in his notes upon Justinian, has furnished a precedent.

In what manner manumission was performed in this country during the first century after the introduction of slavery does not appear: the act of 1668, before mentioned, (76) 76 Ante, p. 36. shews it to have been practised before that period. In 1723 an act was passed, prohibiting the manumission of slaves, upon any pretence whatsoever, except for meritorious services, to be adjudged, and allowed by the governor and council.(77) 77 1723. c. 4. This clause was re-enacted in 1748, and continued to be the law, until after the revolution was accomplished. The number of manumissions under such restrictions must necessarily have been very few. In May 1782 an act passed authorizing, generally, the manumission of slaves, but requiring such as might be set free, not being of sound mind or body, or being above the age of forty-five years, or males under twenty-one, or females under eighteen, to be supported by the person liberating them, or out of his estate. (78) 78 May 1782. c. 21. The act of manumission may be performed either by will, or by deed, under the hand and seal of the party, acknowledged by him, or proved by two witnesses in the court of the county where he resides. There is reason to believe that great numbers have been emancipated since the passing of this act. By the census of 1791 it appears that the number of free Negroes, mulattoes and Indians in Virginia, was then 12,866. It would be a large allowance, to suppose that there were 1800 free Negroes and mulattoes in Virginia when the act took effect; so that upwards of ten thousand must have been indebted to it for their freedom.[18] The number of Indians and their descendants in Virginia at present, is too small to require particular notice. The progress of emancipation in Virginia, is at this time continual, but not rapid; a second census will enable us to form a better judgment of it than at present. The act passed in 1792 accords in some degree with the Justinian code, (79) 79 1794. c. 103. by providing that slaves emancipated may be taken in execution to satisfy any debt contracted by the person emancipating them, before such emancipation is made.[19]

Among the Romans, the *libertini*, or freedmen, were formerly distinguished by a threefold division. (80) 80 Just. Inst. lib. 1. tit. 5. They sometimes obtained what was called the greater liberty, thereby becoming *Roman citizens*. To this privilege, those who were enfranchised by testament, by the census, or by the vindicta, appear to have been alone

17

admitted: sometimes they obtained the lesser liberty only, and became *Latins*; whose condition is thus described by Justinian. "They never enjoyed the right of succession. (81) 81 to estates —For although they led the lives of free men, yet with their last breath they lost both their lives and liberties; for their possessions, like the goods of slaves, were detained by the manumittor." (82) 82 Harris's Inst. lib. 3. tit. 8. Sometimes they obtained only the inferior liberty, being called*dedititii*: such were slaves who had been condemned as criminals, and afterwards obtained manumission through the indulgence of their masters: their conditions was equalled with that of conquered revolters, whom the Romans called, in reproach,*dedititii, quia se suaque omnia dediderunt*: but all these distinctions were abolished by Justinian, (83) 83 Inst. lib. 1. tit. 5. s. 3. by whom all freed men in general were made citizens of Rome, without regard to the form of manumission.—In England, the presenting the villein with *free arms*, seems to have been the symbol of his restoration to all the rights which a feudatory was entitled to. With us, we have seen that emancipation does not confer the rights of citizenship on the person emancipated; on the contrary, both he and his posterity, of the same complexion with himself, must always labour under many civil incapacities. If he is absolved from personal restraint, or corporal punishment, by a master, yet the laws restrain his actions in many instances, where there is none upon a free white man. If he can maintain a suit, he cannot be a witness, a juror, or a judge in any controversy between one of his own complexion and a white person. If he can acquire property in lands, he cannot exercise the right of suffrage, which such a property would confer on his former master; much less can he assist in making those laws by which he is bound. Yet, even under these disabilities, his present condition bears an enviable pre-eminence over his former state. Possessing the liberty of loco-motion, which was formerly denied him, it is in his choice to submit to that civil inferiority, inseparably attached to his condition in this country, or seek some more favourable climate, where all distinctions between men are either totally abolished, or less regarded than in this.

The extirpation of slavery from the United States, is a task equally arduous and momentous. To restore the blessings of liberty to near a million[20] of oppressed individuals, who have groaned under the yoke of bondage, and to their descendants, is an object, which those who trust in Providence, will be convinced would not be unaided by the divine Author of our being, should we invoke his blessing upon our endeavours. Yet human prudence forbids that we should precipitately engage in a work of such hazard as a general and simultaneous emancipation. The mind of man must in some measure be formed for his future condition. The early impressions of obedience and submission, which slaves have received among us, and the no less habitual arrogance and assumption of superiority, among the whites, contribute, equally, to unfit the former for *freedom*, and the latter for *equality*.[21] To expel them all at once, from the United States, would in fact be to devote them only to a lingering death by famine, by disease, and other accumulated miseries: "We have in history but one picture of a similar enterprize, and there we see it was necessary not only to open the sea by a miracle, for them to pass, but more necessary to close it again to prevent their return." (84) 84 Letter from Jas. Sullivan, Esq. to Dr. Belknap. To retain them among us, would be nothing more than to throw so many of the human race upon the earth without the means of subsistence: they would soon become idle, profligate, and miserable. Unfit for their new condition, and unwilling to return to their former laborious course, they would become the caterpillars of the earth, and the tigers of the human race. The recent history of the French West Indies exhibits a melancholy picture of the probable consequences of a general, and momentary emancipation in any of the states, where slavery has made considerable progress. In Massachusetts the abolition of it was effected by a single stroke; a clause in their constitution: (85) [85 Dr. Belknap.] but the whites at that time, were as sixty-five to one, in proportion to the blacks. The whole number of free persons in the United States, south of Delaware state, are 1,233,829, end there are 648,439 slaves; the proportion being less than two to one. Of the cultivators of the earth in the same district, it is probable that there are four slaves for one free white man.——To discharge the former from their present condition, would be attended with an immediate general famine, in those parts of the United States, from which not all the productions of the other states, could deliver them; similar evils might reasonably be apprehended from the adoption of the measure by any one of the southern states; for in all of them the proportion of slaves is too great, not to be attended with calamitous effects, if they were immediately set free.[22] These are serious, I had almost said unsurmountable obstacles, to general, simultaneous emancipation.——There are other considerations not to be disregarded. A great part of the *property* of individuals consists in *slaves*. The laws have sanctioned this species of property. Can the laws take away the property of an individual without his own consent, or without a *just compensation*? Will those who do not hold slaves agree to be taxed to make this compensation? Creditors also, who have trusted their debtors upon the faith of this visible property will be defrauded. If justice demands the emancipation of the slave, she also, *under these circumstances*, seems to plead for the owner, and for his creditor. The claims of nature, it will be said are stronger than those which arise from social institutions, only. I admit it, but nature also dictates to us to provide for our *own* safety, and authorizes all *necessary* measures for that purpose. And we have shewn that our own security, nay, our very existence, might be endangered by the hasty adoption of any measure for the *immediate* relief of the *whole* of this unhappy race. Must we then quit the subject, in despair of the success of any project for the amendment of their, as well as our own, condition? I think not.——Strenuously as I feel my mind opposed to a simultaneous emancipation, for the reasons already mentioned, the abolition of slavery in the United States, and especially in that state, to which I am attached by every tie that nature and society form, is *now* my *first*, and will probably be my last, expiring wish. But here let me avoid the imputation of inconsistency, by observing, that the abolition of slavery may be effected without the *emancipation* of a single slave; without depriving any man of the *property* which he *possesses*, and without defrauding a creditor who has trusted him on the faith of that property. The experiment in that mode has already been begun in some of our sister states. Pennsylvania, under the auspices of the immortal Franklin,[23] begun the work of gradual abolition of slavery in the year 1780, by enlisting nature herself, on the side of humanity. Connecticut followed the example four years after.[24] New-York very lately made an essay which miscarried by a very inconsiderable majority. Mr. Jefferson informs us, that the committee of revisors, of which he was a member, had prepared a bill for the emancipation of all slaves born after passing that act. This is conformable to the Pennsylvania and Connecticut laws.——Why the measure was not brought forward in the general assembly I have never heard. Possibly because objections were foreseen to that part of the bill which relates to the disposal of the blacks, after they had attained a certain age.[25] It certainly seems liable to many, both as to the policy and the practicability of it. To establish such a colony in the territory of the United States, would probably lay the foundation of intestine wars, which would terminate only in their extirpation, or final expulsion. To attempt it in any other quarter of the globe would be attended with the utmost cruelty to the colonists, themselves, and the destruction of their whole race. If the plan were at this moment in operation, it would require the annual exportation of 12,000 persons. This requisite number must, for a series of years be considerably increased, in order to keep pace with the increasing population of those people. In twenty years it would amount to upwards of twenty thousand persons; which is half the number which are now supposed to be annually exported from Africa.—Where would a fund to support this expence be found? Five times the present revenue of the state would barely defray the charge of their passage. Where provisions for their support after their arrival? Where those necessaries which must preserve them from perishing?— Where a territory sufficient to support them?—Or where could they be received as friends, and not as invaders? To colonize them in the United States might seem less difficult. If the territory to be assigned them were beyond the settlements of the whites, would they not be put upon a forlorn hope against the Indians? Would not the expence of transporting them thither, and supporting them, at least for the first and second year, be also far beyond the revenues and abilities of the state? The expence attending a small army in that country hath been found enormous. To transport as many colonists, annually, as we have shewn were necessary to eradicate the evil, would probably require five times as much money as the support of such an army. But the expence would not stop there: they must be assisted and supported at least for another year after their arrival in their new settlements. Suppose them arrived. Illiterate and ignorant as they are, is it probable that they would be capable of instituting such a government, in their new colony, as would be necessary for their own internal happiness, or to secure them from destruction from without? European emigrants, from whatever country they arrive, have been accustomed to the restraint of laws, and to respect for government. These people, accustomed to be ruled with a rod of iron, will not easily submit to milder restraints. They would become hordes of vagabonds, robbers and murderers. Without the aids of an enlightened policy, morality, or religion, what else could be expected from their still savage state, and debased condition?—"But why not retain and *incorporate* the *blacks into the state*?" This question has been well answered by Mr. Jefferson,[26] and who is there so free from prejudices among us, as candidly to declare that he has none against such a measure? The recent scenes transacted in the French colonies in the West Indies are enough to make one shudder with the apprehension of realizing similar calamities in this country. Such probably would be the event of an attempt to smother those prejudices which have been cherished for a period of almost two centuries. Those who secretly favour, whilst they affect to regret, domestic slavery, contend that in abolishing it, we must also abolish that scion from it which I have denominated *civil* slavery. That there must be no distinction of rights; that the descendants of Africans, as men, have an equal claim to all civil rights, as the descendants of Europeans; and upon being delivered from the yoke of bondage have a right to be admitted to all the privileges of a citizen.—But have not men when they enter into a state of society, a right to admit, or exclude any description of persons, as they think proper? If it be true, as Mr. Jefferson seems to suppose, that the Africans are really an inferior race of mankind,[27] will not sound policy advise their exclusion from a society in which they have not yet been admitted to participate in civil rights; and even to guard against such admission, at any future period, since it may eventually depreciate the whole national character? And if prejudices have taken such deep root in our minds, as to render it impossible to eradicate this opinion, ought not so general an error, if it be one, to be respected? Shall we not relieve the necessities of the naked diseased beggar, unless we will invite him to a seat at our table; nor afford him shelter from the inclemencies of the night air, unless we admit him also to share our bed? To deny that we ought to abolish slavery, without incorporating the Negroes into the state, and admitting them to a full participation of all our civil and social rights, appears to me to rest upon a similar foundation. The experiment so far as it has been already made among us, proves that the emancipated blacks are not ambitious of civil rights. To prevent the generation of such an ambition, appears to comport with sound policy; for if it should ever rear its head, its partizans, as well as its opponents, will be enlisted by nature herself, and always ranged in formidable array against each other. We must therefore endeavour to find some middle course, between the tyrannical and iniquitous policy which holds so many human creatures in a state of grievous bondage, and that which would turn loose a numerous, starving, and enraged banditti, upon the innocent descendants of their former oppressors. *Nature*, *time*, and *sound policy* must co-operate with each other to produce such a change: if either be neglected, the work will be incomplete, dangerous, and not improbably destructive.

The plan therefore which I would presume to propose for the consideration of my countrymen is such, as the number of slaves, the difference of their nature, and habits, and the state of agriculture, among us, might render it *expedient*, rather than*desirable* to adopt: and would partake partly of that proposed by Mr. Jefferson, and adopted in other states; and partly of such cautionary restrictions, as a due regard to situation and circumstances, and even to *general* prejudices, might recommend to those, who engage in so arduous, and perhaps unprecedented an undertaking.

1. Let every female born after the adoption of the plan be free, and transmit freedom to all her descendants, both male and female.

2. As a compensation to those persons, in whose families such females, or their descendants may be born, for the expence and trouble of their maintenance during infancy, let them serve such persons until the age of twenty-eight years: let them then receive twenty dollars in money, two suits of clothes, suited to the season, a hat, a pair of shoes, and two blankets. If these things be not voluntarily done, let the county courts enforce the performance, upon complaint.

3. Let all Negroe children be registered with the clerk of the county or corporation court, where born, within one month after their birth: let the person in whose family they are born take a copy of the register, and deliver it to the mother, or if she die to the child, before it is of the age of twenty-one years. Let any Negroe claiming to be free, and above the age of puberty, be considered as of the age of twenty-eight years, if he or she be not registered, as required.

4. Let all such Negroe servants be put on the same footing as white servants and apprentices now are, in respect to food, raiment, correction, and the assignment of their service from one to another.

5. Let the children of Negroes and mulattoes, born in the families of their parents, be bound to service by the overseers of the poor, until they shall attain the age of twenty-one years.—Let all above that age, who are not housekeepers, nor have voluntarily bound themselves to service for a year before the first day of February annually, be then bound for the remainder of the year by the overseers of the poor. Let the overseers of the poor receive fifteen per cent. of their wages, from the person hiring them, as a compensation for their trouble, and ten per cent. per annum out of the wages of such as they may bind apprentices.

6. If at the age of twenty-seven years, the master of a Negroe or mulattoe servant be unwilling to pay his freedom dues, above mentioned, at the expiration of the succeeding year, let him bring him into the county court, clad and furnished with necessaries as before directed, and pay into court five dollars, for the use of the servant, and thereupon let the court direct him to be hired by the overseers of the poor for the succeeding year, in the manner before directed.

7. Let no Negroe or mulattoe be capable of taking, holding, or exercising, any public office, freehold, franchise or privilege, or any estate in lands or tenements, other than a lease not exceeding twenty-one years.—Nor of keeping, or bearing arms,[28] unless authorised so to do by some act of the general assembly, whose duration shall be limitted to three years. Nor of contracting matrimony with any other than a Negroe or mulattoe; nor be an attorney; nor be a juror; nor a witness in any court of judicature, except against; or between Negroes and mulattoes. Nor be an executor or administrator; nor capable of making any will or testament; nor maintain any real action; nor be a trustee of lands or tenements himself, nor any other person to be a trustee to him or to his use.

8. Let all persons born after the passing of the act, be considered as entitled to the same mode of trial in criminal cases, as free Negroes and mulattoes are now entitled to.

The restrictions in this place may appear to favour strongly of prejudice: whoever proposes any plan for the abolition of slavery, will find that he must either encounter, or accommodate himself to prejudice.—I have preferred the latter; not that I pretend to be wholly exempt from it, but that I might avoid as many obstacles as possible to the completion of so desirable a work, as the abolition of slavery. Though I am opposed to the banishment of the Negroes, I wish not to encourage their future residence among us. By denying them the most valuable privileges which civil government affords, I wished to render it their inclination and their interest to seek those privileges in some other climate. There is an immense unsettled territory on this continent[29] more congenial to their natural constitutions than ours, where they may perhaps be received upon more favourable terms than we can permit them to remain with us. Emigrating in small numbers, they will be able to effect settlements more easily than in large numbers; and without the expence or danger of numerous colonies. By releasing them from the yoke of bondage, and enabling them to seek happiness wherever they can hope to find it, we surely confer a benefit, which no one can sufficiently appreciate, who has not tasted of the bitter curse of compulsory servitude. By excluding them from offices, the seeds of ambition would be buried too deep, ever to germinate: by disarming them, we may calm our apprehensions of their resentments arising from past sufferings; by incapacitating them from holding lands, we should add one inducement more to emigration, and effectually remove the foundation of ambition, and party-struggles. Their personal rights, and their property, though limited, would whilst they remain among us be under the protection of the laws; and their condition not at all inferior to that of the *labouring* poor in most other countries. Under such an arrangement we might reasonably hope, that time would either remove from us a race of men, whom we wish not to incorporate with us, or obliterate those prejudices, which now form an obstacle to such incorporation.

But it is not from the want of liberality to the emancipated race of blacks that I apprehend the most serious objections to the plan I have ventured to suggest.—Those slave holders (whose numbers I trust are few) who have been in the habit of considering their fellow creatures as no more than cattle, and the rest of the brute creation, will exclaim that they are to be deprived of their *property*, without compensation. Men who will shut their ears against this moral truth, that all men are by nature *free*, and *equal*, will not even be convinced that they do not possess a *property* in an *unborn* child: they will not distinguish between allowing to *unborn* generations the absolute and unalienable rights of human nature, and taking away that which they *now possess*; they will shut their ears against truth, should you tell them, the loss of the mother's labour for nine months, and the maintenance of a child for a dozen or fourteen years, is amply compensated by the services of that child for as many years more, as he has been an expence to them. But if the voice of reason, justice and humanity be not stifled by sordid avarice, or unfeeling

22

tyranny, it would be easy to convince even those who have entertained such erroneous notions, that the right of one man over another is neither founded in nature, nor in sound policy. That it cannot extend to those *not in being*; that no man can in reality be *deprived* of what he doth not possess: that fourteen years labour by a young person in the prime of life, is an ample compensation for a few months of labour lost by the mother, and for the maintenance of a child, in that coarse homely manner that Negroes are brought up: And lastly, that a state of slavery is not only perfectly incompatible with the principles of government, but with the safety and security of their masters. History evinces this. At this moment we have the most awful demonstrations of it. Shall we then neglect a duty, which every consideration, moral, religious, political, or *selfish*, recommends. Those who wish to postpone the measure, do not reflect that every day renders the task more arduous to be performed. We have now 300,000 slaves among us. Thirty years hence we shall have double the number. In sixty years we shall have 1,200,000. And in less than another century from this day, even that enormous number will be doubled. Milo acquired strength enough to carry an ox, by beginning with the ox while he was yet a calf. If we complain that the calf is too heavy for our shoulders, what will not the ox be?

To such as apprehend danger to our agricultural interest, and the depriving the families of those whose principal reliance is upon their slaves, of support, it will be proper to submit a view of the gradual operation, and effects of this plan. They will no doubt be surprized to hear, that whenever it is adopted, the number of slaves will not be diminished for forty years after it takes place; that it will even encrease for thirty years; that at the distance of sixty years, there will be one-third of the number at its first commencement: that it will require *above a century* to complete it; and that the number of blacks *under twenty-eight*, and consequently bound to service, in the families they are born in, will always be at least as great, as the present number of slaves. These circumstances I trust will remove many objections, and that they are truly stated will appear upon enquiry.[30] It will further appear, that females only will arrive at the age of emancipation within the first forty-five years; all the males during that period, continuing either in slavery, or bound to service till the age of twenty-eight years. The earth cannot want cultivators, whilst our population increases as at present, and three-fourths of those employed therein are held to service, and the remainder compellable to labour. For we must not lose sight of this important consideration, that these people must be *bound* to labour, if they do not *voluntarily*engage therein. Their faculties are at present only calculated for that object; if they be not employed therein they will become drones of the worst description. In absolving them from the yoke of slavery, we must not forget the interests of the society. Those interests require the exertions of every individual in some mode or other; and those who have not wherewith to support themselves honestly without corporal labour, whatever be their complexion, ought to be compelled to labour. This is the case in England, where domestic slavery has long been unknown. It must also be the case in every well ordered society; and where the numbers of persons without property increase, there the coertion of the laws becomes more immediately requisite. The proposed plan would necessarily have this effect, and therefore ought to be accompanied with such a regulation. Though the rigours of our police in respect to this unhappy race ought to be softened, yet, its regularity, and punctual administration should be increased, rather than relaxed. If we doubt the propriety of such measures, what must we think of the situation of our country, when instead of 300,000, we shall have more than *two millions* of SLAVES among us? This *must happen within a* CENTURY, if we do not set about the abolition of slavery. Will not our posterity curse the days of their nativity with all the anguish of Job? Will they not execrate the memory of those ancestors, who, having it in their power to avert evil, have, like their first parents, entailed a curse upon all future generations? We know that the rigour of the laws respecting slaves unavoidably must increase with their numbers: What a blood-stained code must that be which is calculated for the restraint of *millions* held in bondage! Such must our unhappy country exhibit within a century, unless we are both wise and just enough to avert from posterity the calamity and reproach, which are otherwise unavoidable.

I am not vain enough to presume the plan I have suggested entirely free from objection; nor that in offering my own ideas on the subject, I have been more fortunate than others: but from the communication of sentiment between those who lament the evil, it is possible that an effectual remedy may at length be discovered. Whenever that happens the golden age of our country will begin. Till then,

———*Non hospes ab hospite tutus,*
Non Herus à Familie: fratrum quoque gratia rara.

THE END.

Footnotes

[1] The subject of a preceding Lecture, with which the present was immediately connected, was, An Enquiry into the Rights of Persons, as Citizens of the United States of America.

[2] The American standard, at the commencement of those hostilities which terminated in the revolution, had these words upon it———AN APPEAL TO HEAVEN!

[3] The Author here takes the liberty of making his acknowledgments to the reverend Jeremiah Belknap, D. D. of Boston, and to Zephaniah Swift, Esq. representative in congress from Connecticut, for their obliging communications; he hath occasionally made use of them in several parts of this Lecture, where he may have omitted referring to them.

[4] Dr. Belknap's answers to St. G. T.'s queries.

[5] Letter from Zephaniah Swift to St. G. T.

[6] The Constitution of Virginia, art. 7. declares, that the right of suffrage shall remain as then exercised: the act of 1723, c. 4 (edit. 1733,), sect. 23, declared, that no Negroe, mulattoe, or Indian, shall have any vote at the election of burgesses, or any other election whatsoever.—This act, it is presumed, was in force at the adoption of the constitution.—The act of 1785, c. 55 (edit. of 1794, c. 17,), also expressly excludes them from the right of suffrage.

[7] These arguments are, in fact, borrowed from the Spirit of Laws.

[8] "About the same time (the reign of queen Elizabeth) a traffic in the human species, called Negroes, was introduced into England, which is one of the most odious and unnatural branches of trade the sordid and avaricious mind of mortals ever invented.—It had been carried on before this period by Genoese traders, who bought a patent from Charles the fifth, containing an exclusive right of carrying Negroes from the Portuguese settlements in Africa, to America and the West Indies; but the English nation had not yet engaged in the iniquitous traffic.—One William Hawkins, an expert English seaman, having made several voyages to the coast of Guinea, and from thence to Brazil and the West Indies, had acquired considerable knowledge of the countries. At his death he left his journals with his son, John Hawkins, in which he described the lands of America and the West Indies as exceedingly rich and fertile, but utterly neglected for want of hands to improve them. He represented the natives of Europe as unequal to the task in such a scorching climate; but those of Africa as well adapted to undergo the labours requisite. Upon which John Hawkins immediately formed a design of transporting Africans into the western world; and having drawn a plan for the execution of it, he laid it

before some of his opulent neighbours for encouragement and approbation. To them it appeared promising and advantageous. A subscription was opened and speedily filled up, by Sir Lionel Ducket, Sir Thomas Lodge, Sir William Winter, and others, who plainly perceived the vast profits that would result from such a trade. Accordingly three ships were fitted out, and manned by an hundred select sailors, whom Hawkins encouraged to go with him by promises of good treatment and great pay. In the year 1562 he set sail for Africa, and in a few weeks arrived at the country called Sierra Leona, where he began his commerce with the Negroes. While he trafficked with them, he found the means of giving them a charming description of the country to which he was bound; the unsuspicious Africans listened to him with apparent joy and satisfaction, and seemed remarkably fond of his European trinkets, food, and clothes. He pointed out to them the barrenness of the country, and their naked and wretched condition, and promised if any of them were weary of their miserable circumstances, and would go along with him, he would carry them to a plentiful land, where they should *live happy*, and *receive* an abundant *recompence* for their labours. He told them the country was inhabited by such men as himself and his jovial companions, and *assured* them of *kind usage* and *great friendship*. In short, the Negroes were overcome by his flattering promises, and *three hundred* stout fellows accepted his offer, and consented to embark along with him. Every thing being settled on the most amicable terms between them, Hawkins made preparations for his voyage. But in the night before his departure his Negroes were attacked by a large body from a different quarter; Hawkins, being alarmed with the shrieks and cries of dying persons, ordered his men to the assistance of his slaves, and having surrounded the assailants, carried a number of them on board as prisoners of war. The next day he set sail for Hispaniola with his cargo of human creatures; but during the passage, he treated the prisoners of war in a different manner from his volunteers. Upon his arrival he disposed of his cargo to great advantage; and endeavoured to inculcate on the Spaniards who bought the negroes the same distinction to be observed: but they having *purchased all at the same rate*, considered them as slaves of the same condition, and consequently treated all alike."

Hawkins having returned to England, soon after made preparations for a second voyage. "In his passage he fell in with the Minion man of war, which accompanied him to the Coast of Africa. After his arrival he began as formerly to traffic with the Negroes, endeavouring by persuasions and *prospects* of *reward*, to induce them to go along with him—but now they were more reserved and jealous of his designs, and as none of their neighbours had returned, they were apprehensive he had killed and eat them. The crew of the man of war observing the Africans backward and suspicious, began to laugh at his gentle and dilatory methods of proceeding, and proposed having immediate recourse to force and compulsion—but Hawkins considered it as cruel and unjust, and tried by persuasions, promises and threats, to prevail on them to desist from a purpose so unwarrantable and barbarous. In vain did he urge his authority and instructions from the Queen: the bold and headstrong sailors would hear of no restraints. Drunkenness and avarice are deaf to the voice of humanity. They pursue their violent design, and, after several unsuccessful attacks, in which *many* of them lost their *lives*, the cargo was at length compleated by barbarity and force.

"Hence arose that horrid and inhuman practice of dragging Africans into slavery, which has since been *so* pursued, in defiance of every principle of justice and religion. Had Negroes been brought from the flames, to which in some countries they were devoted on their falling prisoners of war, and in others, sacrificed at the funeral obsequies of the great and powerful among themselves; in short had they by this traffic been delivered from *torture* or *death*, European merchants *might have some excuse* to plead in its vindication. *But according to the common mode in which it has been conducted*, we must confess it a difficult matter to conceive a *single* argument in its defence. And though policy has given countenance and sanction to the trade, yet every candid and impartial man must confess, that it is atrocious and unjustifiable in every light in which it can be viewed, and turns merchants into a band of robbers, and trade into atrocious acts of fraud and violence." Historical Account of South-Carolina and Georgia. Anonymous. London printed in 1779—page 20, &c.

"The number of Negroe slaves bartered for in one year (viz. 1768), on the Coast of Africa from Cape Blanco, to Rio Congo, amounted to 104,000 souls, whereof more than half (viz. 53,000) were shipped on account of British merchants, and 6,300 on the account of British Americans." The Law of Retribution by Granville Sharpe, Esq. page 147. note.

[9] See the various tracts on this subject, by Granville Sharpe, Esq. of London.

[10] The condition of a *villein* had most of the incidents I have before described in giving the idea of *slavery*, in general. His services were uncertain and indeterminate, such as his lord thought fit to require; or as some of our ancient writers express it, he knew not in the evening what he was to do in the morning, he was bound to do whatever he was commanded. He was liable to beating, imprisonment, and every other chastisement his lord could devise, except killing and maiming. He was incapable of acquiring property for his own benefit; he was himself the subject of property; as such saleable and transmissible. If he was a villein regardant he passed with the land to which he was annexed, but might be severed at the will of his lord; if he was a villein in gross, he was an hereditament, or a chattel real, according to his lord's interest; being descendible to the heir, where the lord was absolute *owner*, and transmissible to the executor where the lord had only a term of years in him. Lastly, the slavery extended to the issue, if the father was a villein, our law deriving the condition of the child from that of the father, contrary to the Roman law, in which the rule was, *partus sequitur ventum.* Hargrave's Case of Negroe Somerset, page 26 and 27.

The same writer refers the origin of vassalage in England, principally to the wars between the British, Saxon, Danish, and Norman nations, contending for the sovereignty of that country, in opposition to the opinion of judge Fitzherbert, who supposes villeinage to have commenced at the conquest. Ib. 27, 28. And this he proves from Spelman and other antiquaries. Ib. The writ *de nativo habendo*, by which the lord was enabled to recover his villein that had absconded from him, creates a presumption that all the natives of England were at some period reduced to a state of villeinage, the word *nativus*, which signified a villein, most clearly designating the person meant thereby to be a *native*: this etymon is obvious, as well from the import of the word *nativus*, as from the history of the more remote ages of Britain. Sir Edward Coke's Etymology, "*quia plerumque nascuntur servi*," is one of those puerile conceits, which so frequently occur in his works, and are unworthy of so great a man.

Barrington in his observations upon *magna carta* c. 4. observes, that the villeins who held by servile tenures were considered as so many negroes on a sugar plantation; the words "*liber homo*," in magna carta, c. 14. with all deference to sir Edward Coke, who says they mean a *free-holder*, I understand as meaning *a free man*,[Liber homo, &c. the title of *freeman* was formerly *confined* to the *nobility* and *gentry* who were *descended* of free ancestors.—Burgh's Political Disquisitions, vol. iii. p. 400, who cites Spelman's Glossary, voc. Liber homo.] as contradistinguished from a *villein*: for in the very next sentence the words "et *villanus* alterius quam noster," occur. Villeins must certainly have been numerous at that day, to have obtained a place in the Great Charter. It is no less an evidence that their condition was in a state of melioration.

26

In Poland, at this day, the peasants seem to be in an absolute state of slavery, or at least of villeinage, to the nobility, who are the land-holders.

[11] Among the Israelites, according to the Mosaical law, "If a man smote his servant, or his maid, with a rod, and he died under his hand, he should surely be punished—notwithstanding if he continue a day or two, he should not be punished [Exod. c. 21]:" for, saith the text, he is *his money*. Our legislators appear to have adopted the reason of the latter clause, without the humanity of the former part of the law.

[12] Hannah and other Indians, against Davis.—Since this adjudication, I have met with a manuscript act of assembly made in 1691 c. 9 entitled, "An Act for a free Trade with Indians," the enacting clause of which is in the very words of the act of 1705. c. 52. A similar title to an act of that session occurs in the edition of 1733. p. 94. and the chapter is numbered as in the manuscript. If this manuscript be authentic (which there is some reason to presume, it being copied in some blank leaves at the end of Purvis's edition, and apparently written about the time of the passage of the act), it would seem that no Indians brought into Virginia for more than a century, nor any of their descendents, can be retained in slavery in this commonwealth.

[13] Although it be true that the number of slaves in the *whole* state bears the proportion of 292,427, to 747,610, the whole number of souls in the state, that is, nearly as *two* to *five*; yet this proportion is by no means *uniform* throughout the state. In the forty-four counties lying upon the Bay, and the great rivers of the state, and comprehended by a line including Brunswick, Cumberland, Goochland, Hanover, Spottsylvania, Stafford, Prince William and Fairfax, and the counties eastward thereof, the number of slaves is 196,542, and the number of free persons, including free Negroes and mulattoes, 198,371 only. So that the blacks in that populous and extensive district of country are *more numerous* than the whites. In the second class, comprehending nineteen counties, and extending from the last mentioned line to the Blue Ridge, and including the populous counties of Frederick and Berkeley, beyond the Blue Ridge, there are 82,286 slaves, and 136,251 free persons; the number of free persons in that class not being two to one, to the slaves. In the third class the proportion is considerably increased; the eleven counties of which it consists contain only 11,218 slaves, and 76,281 free persons. This class reaches to the Allegany ridge of mountains: the fourth and last class, comprehending fourteen counties westward of the third class, contains only 2,381 slaves, and 42,288 free persons. It is obvious from this statement that almost all the dangers and inconveniences which may be apprehended from a state of slavery on the one hand, or an attempt to abolish it, on the other, will be confined to the people eastward of the blue ridge of mountains.

[14] The following is a list of the acts, or titles of acts, imposing duties on slaves imported, which occur in the various compilations of our laws, or in the Sessions Acts, or Journals.

699,	c. 12. title only retained. Edit. of 1733,	. 113	f
701,	c. 5. the same,	16	1
704,	c. 4. the same,	22	1
705,	c. 1. the same,	26	1
710,	c. 1. the same,	39	(
	c. 3. the same,		(

[15] ☞ The following extract from a petition to the throne, presented from the house of burgesses of Virginia, April 1, 1772, will shew the sense of the people of Virginia on the subject of slavery at that period.

"The many instances of your majesty's benevolent intentions and more gracious disposition to promote the prosperity and happiness of your subjects in the colonies, encourages us to look up to the throne, and implore your majesty's paternal assistance in averting a calamity of a most alarming nature."

"The importation of slaves into the colonies from the coast of Africa hath long been considered as a trade of great inhumanity, and under its *present encouragement*, we have too much reason to fear *will endanger the very existence* of your majesty's American dominions."

"We are sensible that some of your majesty's subjects of *Great Britain* may reap emoluments from this sort of traffic, but when we consider that it greatly retards the settlement of the colonies, with *more useful* inhabitants, and may, in time, have the most destructive influence, we presume to hope that the *interest of a few* be disregarded when placed in competition with the security and happiness of such numbers of your majesty's dutiful and loyal subjects."

"Deeply impressed with these sentiments, we most humbly beseech your majesty to *remove all those restraints* on your majesty's governors of this colony, *which inhibit their assenting to such laws as might check so very pernicious a commerce.*" Journals of the House of Burgesses, page 131.

This petition produced no effect, as appears from the first clause of ourCONSTITUTION, where among other acts of misrule, "the inhuman use of the royal negative" in refusing us permission to exclude slaves from among us by law, is enumerated, among the reasons for *separating from Great Britain.*

[16] In December term 1788, one John Huston was tried in the general court for the murder of a slave; the jury found him guilty of manslaughter, and the court, upon a motion in arrest of judgment, discharged him without any punishment. The general assembly being then sitting, some of the members of the court mentioned the case to some leading characters in the legislature, and the act was at the same session repealed.

[17] See Jefferson's Notes, 259.—The Marquis de Chatelleux's Travels, I have not noted the page; the Law of Retribution, by Granville Sharpe, pa. 151, 238, notes. The Just Limitation of Slavery, by the same author; pa. 15, note. Ibidem, pa. 33, 50, Ib. Append. No. 2. Encyclopédie. Tit. Esclave. Laws of Barbadoes, &c.

[18] There are *more* free Negroes and mulattoes in Virginia alone, than are to be found in the four New-England states, and Vermont in addition to them. The progress of emancipation in this state is therefore much greater than our *Eastern* brethren may at first suppose. There are only 1087 free Negroes and mulattoes in the States of New-York, New-Jersey and Pennsylvania, *more*, than in Virginia. Those who take a subject in the gross, have little idea of the result of an exact scrutiny. Out of 20,348 inhabitants on the Eastern Shore of Virginia 1185 were free Negroes and mulattoes when the census was taken. The number is since much augmented.

[19] The act of 1795. c. 11. enacts, that any person held in slavery may make complaint to a magistrate, or to the court of the district county or corporation wherein he resides, and not elsewhere. The magistrate, if the complaint be made to him, shall issue his warrant to summon the owner before him, and compel him to give bond and security to suffer the complainant to appear at the next court to petition the court to be admitted to sue *in forma pauperis.* If the owner refuse, the magistrate shall order the complainant into the custody of the officer serving the warrant, at the expence of the master, who shall keep him until the sitting of the court, and then produce him before it. Upon petition to the court, if the court be satisfied as to the material facts, they shall assign the complainant council, who shall state the facts with his opinion thereon to the court; and unless from the circumstances so stated, and the opinion thereon given, the court shall *see manifest reason to deny their interference*, they shall order the clerk to issue process against the owner, and the complainant shall remain in the custody of the sheriff until the owner shall give bond and security to have him forthcoming to answer the judgment of the court. And by the general law in case of pauper's suits; the complainants shall have writs of subpoena gratis; and by the practice of the courts, he is permitted to attend the taking the depositions of witnesses, and go and come freely to and from court, for the prosecution of his suit.

[20] The number of slaves in the United States at the time of the late census, was something under 700,000.

29

[21] Mr. Jefferson most forcibly paints the unhappy influence on the manners of the people produced by the existence of slavery among us. The whole commerce between master and slave, says he, is a perpetual exercise of the most boisterous passions, the most unremitting despotism on the one part, and degrading submissions on the other. Our children see this, and learn to imitate it; for man is an imitative animal. This quality is the germ of education in him. From his cradle to his grave he is learning what he sees others do. If a parent had no other motive either in his own philanthropy or his self love, for restraining the intemperance of passion towards his slave, it should always be a sufficient one that his child is present. But generally it is not sufficient. The parent storms, the child looks on, catches the lineaments of wrath, puts on the same airs in the circle of smaller slaves, gives a loose to his worst of passions; and thus nursed, educated, and daily exercised in tyranny, cannot but be stamped by it with odious peculiarities. The man must be a prodigy who can retain his manners and morals undepraved by such circumstances. And with what execrations would the statesman be loaded, who permitting one half the citizens thus to trample on the rights of the other, transforms them into despots, and these into enemies, destroys the morals of the one part, and the amor patriæ of the other. For if a slave can have a country in this world, it must be any other in preference to that in which he is born to live and labour for another; in which he must lock up the faculties of his nature, contribute as far as depends on his individual endeavours to the evanishment of the human race, or entail his own miserable condition on the endless generations proceeding from him. With the morals of the people, their industry also, is destroyed. For in a warm climate, no man will labour for himself who can make another labour for him. This is so true, that of the proprietors of slaves a very small proportion indeed are ever seen to labour. And can the liberties of a nation be ever thought secure when we have removed their only firm basis, a conviction in the minds of the people, that these liberties are of the gift of God? That they are not to be violated but with his wrath? Indeed I tremble for my country when I reflect that God is just: that his justice cannot sleep for ever: that considering numbers, nature, and natural means only, a revolution of the wheel of fortune, an exchange of situation is among possible events: that it may become probable by supernatural interference! The Almighty has no attribute which can take side with us in such a contest.—But it is impossible to be temperate and to pursue this subject through the various considerations of policy, of morals, of history, natural and civil. We must be contented to hope they will force their way into every one's mind. I think a change already perceptible, since the origin of the present revolution. The spirit of the master is abating, that of the slave rising from the dust; his condition mollifying; the way I hope preparing, under the auspices of Heaven, for a total emancipation, and that this is disposed in the order of events, to be with the consent of their masters, rather than by their extirpation. Notes on Virginia, 298.

[22] What is here advanced is not to be understood as implying an opinion that the labour of slaves is more productive than that of freemen.—The author of the Treatise on the Wealth of Nations, informs us, "That it appears from the experience of all ages and nations, that the work done by freemen comes cheaper in the end than that done by slaves. That it is found to do so, even in Boston, New-York and Philadelphia, where the wages of common labour are very high." Vol. 1. pa. 123. Lond. edit. oct. Admitting this conclusion, it would not remove the objection that emancipated slaves would not willingly labour.

[23] Doctor Franklin, it is said, drew the bill for the gradual abolition of slavery in Pennsylvania.

[24] It is probable that similar laws have been passed in some other states; but I have not been able to procure a note of them.

[25] The object of the amendment proposed to be offered to the legislature, was to emancipate all slaves born after a certain period; and further directing that they should continue with their parents to a certain age, then be brought up, at the public expence, to tillage, arts, or sciences, according to their geniuses, till the females should be eighteen, and the males twenty-one years of age, when they should be colonized to such a place as the circumstances of the time should render most proper; sending them out with arms, implements of household and of the handicraft arts, seeds, pairs of the useful domestic animals, &c. to declare them a free and independent people, and extend to them our alliance and protection, till they shall have acquired strength; and to send vessels at the same time to other parts of the world for an equal number of white inhabitants; to induce whom to migrate hither, proper encouragements should be proposed. Notes on Virginia, 251.

[26] It will probably be asked, why not retain the blacks among us and *incorporate them into the state*? Deep-rooted prejudices entertained by the whites; ten thousand recollections by the blacks, of the injuries they have sustained; new provocations; the *real distinctions* which *nature* has made; and many other circumstances will divide us into parties and produce convulsions, which will probably never end but in the extermination of one or the other race. To these objections which are political may be added others which are physical and moral. The first difference which strikes us is that of colour.—&c. The circumstance of superior beauty is thought worthy attention in the propagation of our horses, dogs, and other domestic animals; Why not in that of man? &c. In general their existence appears to participate more of sensation than reflection. Comparing them by their faculties of memory, reason and imagination, it appears to me that in memory they are equal to the whites; in reason much inferior; that in imagination they are dull, tasteless and anamolous. &c. The improvement of the blacks in body and mind, in the first instance of their mixture with the whites, has been observed by every one, and proves that their inferiority is not the effect merely of their condition of life. We know that among the Romans, about the Augustan age, especially, the condition of their slaves was much more deplorable, than that of the blacks on the continent of America. Yet among the Romans their slaves were often their rarest artists. They excelled too in science, insomuch as to be usually employed as tutors to their masters' children. Epictetus, Terence, and Phoedrus were slaves. But they were of the race of whites. It is not their condition then, but nature, which has produced the distinction. The opinion that they are inferior in the faculties of reason and imagination, must be hazarded with great diffidence. To justify a general conclusion requires many observations. &c.—I advance it therefore as a suspicion only, that the blacks, whether originally a distinct race, or made distinct by time and circumstances, are inferior to the whites both in the endowments of body and mind. &c. This unfortunate difference of colour, and perhaps of faculty, is a powerful obstacle to the emancipation of these people. Among the Romans emancipation required but one effort. The slave, when made free, might mix with, without staining, the blood of his master. But with us a second is necessary, unknown to history.—See the passage at length, Notes on Virginia, page 252 to 265.

"In the present case, it is not only the slave who is beneath his master, it is the Negroe who is beneath the white man. No act of enfranchisement can efface this unfortunate distinction." Chatelleux's Travels in America.

[27] The celebrated David Hume, in his Essay on National Character, advances the same opinion; Doctor Beattie, in his Essay on Truth, controverts it with many powerful

31

arguments. Early prejudices, had we more satisfactory information than we can possibly possess on the subject at present, would render an inhabitant of a country where Negroe slavery prevails, an improper umpire between them.

[28] See Spirit of Laws, 12-15.——1. Black Com. 417.

[29] The immense territory of Louisiana, which extends as far south as the lat. 25° and the two Floridas, would probably afford a ready asylum for such as might choose to become Spanish subjects. How far their political rights might be enlarged in these countries, is, however questionable: but the climate is undoubtedly more favourable to the African constitution than ours, and from this cause, it is not improbable that emigrations from these states would in time be very considerable.

[30] As it may not be unacceptable to some readers to observe the operation of this plan, I shall subjoin the following statement:

PRELIMINARY REMARKS.

1. The number of slaves in Virginia by the late census being found to be 292,427, they may now, in round numbers be estimated at   300,000.

2. Let it be supposed that the males and females are nearly or altogether equal in number.

3. According to Dr. Franklin, the people of America double their numbers in about twenty-eight years; and according to Mr. Jefferson, the negroes increase as fast as the whites, they will therefore double, at least every thirty years.

4. Let it be supposed that in thirty years one half of the present race of negroes will be extinct.

5. Let it be supposed that in forty-five years there will not remain more than one-fifth of the present race alive.

6. Let it be likewise supposed, that in sixty years the whole of the present race will be extinct.

7. For conciseness sake, let the present race be called *ante-nati*, those born after the adoption of the plan, *post-nati*.

FROM HENCE IT WILL FOLLOW,

1. That the present number of slaves being   300,000.

2. In thirty years their numbers will amount to   600,000.

3. But at that period as one half of them will be extinct, (rem. 4.) their numbers will stand thus:

Ante-nati,   150,000

Post-nati,   450,000

                        ———   600,

000.

4. The mean increase of the post-nati for the next thirty years will therefore be 450000/30, annually, or   15,0 00.

5. If one half of these be males, who are still to remain slaves, there will in the first sixteen years, be born   120, 000.

6. After the first sixteen years, the post-nati females will begin to breed; the proportion of males born to slavery in the next twelve years may be estimated at one-fourth of the whole number born after the commencement of that period. Their number will be   52,0 00.

7. The number of *slaves* living in Virginia at the end of *thirty* years from the adoption of the plan, will be,

ante-nati (prop. 3.)	150,000	
Post-nati males born in the first 16 years,	120,000	
Post-nati males born in the last 12 years,	52,500	
	————	322, 500.

8. The number of *negroes* at the same time will stand thus:

Slaves,	322,500	
Post-nati free born,	277,500	
	————	600, 000.

9. After twenty-eight years from the first adoption, this plan of gradual emancipation will first begin to manifest its effects, by the complete emancipation of one twenty-eighth part of the post-nati free born during that period each succeeding year, for twenty-eight years more; their numbers will be, 277500/28, or   9,91 0.

These will be all females.

10. It being admitted that the negroes double every thirty years, the supposition that in forty-five years, their numbers will be half as many more as in thirty, will not be very erroneous, if so, the whole race of them at that period will be   900, 000.

11. Their numbers will stand thus:

Ante-nati,	60,000	
Post-nati,	840,000	
	————	600, 000.

12. After twenty-eight years are past, the number of slaves born must continually diminish. Suppose their number born in the last 17 years, to be   13,1 25.

33

one-fourth as many as those born in the preceding twelve years, they will be 52500/4, or

13. The slaves in Virginia in forty-five years will then be,

ante-nati,	60,000
Post-nati males born in the first sixteen years,	120,000
Ditto, born in the next twelve years,	52,500
Ditto, born in the last seventeen years,	13,125

245,625.

At this period the emancipation of males will begin.

14. But after twenty eight years it has been shewn that 9,910 negroes will annually arrive at the age of emancipation, their whole number in forty-five years will be

168,470.

15. The state of the negroes at the end of 45 years, will then be,

slaves,	245,625
Post-nati fully emancipated (females),	168,470
Post-nati not emancipated,	485,905

900,000.

16. In sixty years the whole number of negroes will be

1,200,000.

17. At that period the whole of the present race will be extinct; and we may also infer that one half of those born in the first thirty years will be also extinct; the number of slaves born in that period has been shewn, (prop. 7.) to be 172,500, the number of these then living will be 172,500/2, or

86,250.

18. One half of the post-nati free born, during that period, being now fully emancipated, may be likewise presumed to be extinct; their numbers (prop. 8.) will be, 277,500/2, or

138,750.

19. The state of the negroes at the end of sixty years, will therefore be:

Slaves born during the first thirty years,	86,250
Ditto born after that period,	13,125
Post-nati fully emancipated,	138,750
Post-nati under 28 years of age,	961,875

1,200,000.

20. At the end of ninety years the number of negroes will be

2,40

34

0,000.

21. Of this number, those only born after the first thirty years, being   13,1
supposed to be living, the number of slaves (prop. 12) will then be reduced to   25.

22. And as the last mentioned number of slaves are supposed to be born
within forty-five years, their whole number will be extinct in fifteen years
more, that is, in *one hundred* and *five* years from the first adoption of the plan.

23. By prop. 19. it appears, that out of 1,200,000 negroes, there will then
be 961,875 under the age of twenty-eight years, the period of emancipation.

24. We may therefore conclude, that from *two-thirds* to *three-fourths* of the
whole number of blacks will *always* be liable to service.

Printed in Great Britain
by Amazon

37005282R00030